PRE-ACCREDITATION
MATHS & LITERACY FOR
BEAUTY THERAPY

Graduated exercises and practice exam

Andrew Spencer

A+ National Pre-accreditation Maths & Literacy for Beauty Therapy
1st Edition
Andrew Spencer

Publishing editors: Jane Moylan and Jana Raus
Editor: Kerry Nagle
Senior designer: Vonda Pestana
Cover design: Vonda Pestana
Text design: Vonda Pestana
Cover image: iStockphoto
Photo research: UC Publishing
Production controller: Jo Vraca and Damian Almeida
Typeset by UC Publishing Pty Ltd

Any URLs contained in this publication were checked for currency during the production process. Note, however, that the publisher cannot vouch for the ongoing currency of URLs.

Acknowledgements
We would like to thank the following for permission to reproduce copyright material:

iStockphotos: p2 ivanmateev,p4 leezsnow, p5 ZoiaKostina, p8 ivanmateev, p10 lovleah, p11 kovalvs, p12 samaneh_kh, p14 left leventince, p14 right Gubcio, p16 left lostinbirds, p16 right ploveking, p17 KlJem, p18 AR-tem, p20 Nick_Thompson, p21 hidesy, p23 LdF, p25 Hanis,p26 Anyka, p29 Vlingva, p30 Hightower_NRW, p33 Gordo25.

For product information and technology assistance,
in Australia call **1300 790 853**;
in New Zealand call **0800 449 725**

For permission to use material from this text or product, please email
aust.permissions@cengage.com

ISBN 978 0 170 46238 9

Cengage Learning Australia
Level 7, 80 Dorcas Street
South Melbourne, Victoria Australia 3205

Cengage Learning New Zealand
Unit 4B Rosedale Office Park
331 Rosedale Road, Albany, North Shore 0632, NZ

For learning solutions, visit **cengage.com.au**

Printed in Australia by Ligare Pty Limited.
1 2 3 4 5 6 7 14 13 12 11 10

A+ National
PRE-ACCREDITATION
Maths & Literacy for Beauty Therapy

Contents

Introduction

It has always been important to understand, from a teacher's perspective, the nature of the mathematical skills students need for their future, rather than teaching them textbook mathematics. This has been a guiding principle behind the development of the content in this workbook. To teach maths that is *relevant* to students seeking apprenticeships is the best that we can do, to give students an education in the field that they would like to work in.

The content in this resource is aimed at the level that is needed for a student to have the best possibility of improving their maths and literacy skills specifically for Beauty Therapy. Students can use this workbook to prepare for an entry assessment, or even to assist with basic numeracy and literacy at the VET/TAFE level. Coupled with the NelsonNet website, https://www.nelsonnet.com.au/free-resources, these resources have the potential to improve the students' understanding of basic mathematical concepts that can be applied to trades. These resources have been trialled, and they work.

Commonly used trade terms are introduced so that students have a basic understanding of terminology they will encounter in the workplace environment. Students who can complete this workbook and reach an 80 per cent or higher outcome in all topics will have achieved the goal of this resource. These students will go on to complete work experience, do a VET accredited course, or be able to gain entry into VET/TAFE or an apprenticeship in the trade of their choice.

The content in this workbook is the first step towards bridging the gap between what has been learnt in previous years, and what needs to be remembered and re-learnt for use in trades. Students will significantly benefit from the consolidation of the basic maths and literacy concepts.

Every school has students who want to work with their hands, and not all students want to go to university. The best students want to learn what they don't know, and if students want to learn, then this book has the potential to give them a good start in life.

This resource has been specifically tailored to prepare students for sitting VET/TAFE admission tests, and for giving students the basic skills they will need for a career in trade. In many ways, it is a win-win situation, with students enjoying and studying relevant maths for work and VET/TAFE receiving students that have improved basic maths and literacy skills.

All that is needed is patience, hard work, a positive attitude, a belief in yourself that you can do it and a desire to achieve. The rest is up to you.

About the author

Andrew Spencer has studied education both within Australia and overseas. He has a Bachelor of Education, as well as a Masters of Science in which he specialised in teacher education. Andrew has extensive experience in teaching secondary mathematics throughout New South Wales and South Australia for well over fifteen years. He has taught a range of subject areas including Maths, English, Science, Classics, Physical Education and Technical Studies. His sense of the importance of practical mathematics continued to develop with the range of subject areas he taught in.

Acknowledgements

For Paula, Zach, Katelyn, Mum and Dad.

Many thanks to Mal Aubrey (GTA) and all training organisations for their input.

To the De La Salle Brothers for their selfless work with all students.

Thanks also to Dr. Pauline Carter for her unwavering support for all maths teachers.

This is for all students who value learning, who are willing to work hard and who have character … and are characters!

Unit 1: Spelling

Short-answer questions

Specific instructions to students

- This is an exercise to help you to identify and correct spelling errors.
- Read the activity below, then answer accordingly.

Read the following passage and identify and correct the spelling errors:

Aldo the beauty sallon manager arrives at 9.00 a.m. on Friday morning and the customers begin to arive at 9.10 a.m. There are three beauty therapasts proparing for a busy day as Friday is ussually one of the buisiest days of the week. Many curstomers have heard of the new store opening and are keen to try the services. Aldo breifly meets with the staff and explains that a few of the OHWS preceedures have not been adheard too. One therapist in particular had forgottan to sterilise equiptment. This was a major health hasard. No treatmeants could be undertaken without all of the OHWS regalations being met. This was quikly completed.

Three customers wanted a lash and bruw treatment, a slimming body wrap and a deluxe facial. Two other customers required manecures and one other customer wanted a peercing. Aldo was out the back of the salon when three more customers entered, hoping to book a time for nail enhansements. Aldo booked in the customers for the 10.00 a.m. time slot.

Incorrect words:

_____

_____

Correct words:

_____

_____

Unit 2: Alphabetising

Short-answer questions

Specific instructions to students

- In this unit, you will be able to practise your alphabetising skills.
- Read the activity below, then answer accordingly.

Put the following words into alphabetical order:

manicure	aromatherapy
nails	facial
nail enhancement	body treatment
pedicure	lash and brow
piercings	wax
epilating	make-up
massage	beauty services

Answer:

_____

_____

_____

_____

_____

_____

_____

_____

_____

_____

_____

_____

_____

_____

Short-answer questions

Specific instructions to students

- This is an exercise to help you understand what you read.
- Read the following activity, then answer the questions that follow.

Read the following passage and answer the questions in sentence form.

Jill, the manager of the beauty salon, knew that Friday would be a busy day as they were totally booked out. She arrived at 7.45 a.m. to prepare for the customers that were booked in. One of her staff had called in sick, leaving four staff to work in the salon. Unfortunately, her relieving staff was also sick so there would only be four staff to work. The day was going to be hectic! Phillipa arrived soon after Jill and immediately began by setting up the work stations and placing out the towels and equipment. Once she had finished setting up, the first customers entered the salon.

Caryle and Tate, who were also staff members, arrived and Jill was grateful that all of her staff members were now present. The first customer that Caryle tended to required a half leg wax and the following three customers that she met wanted piercings. Rhiannon and Carlene entered the salon for their 9.45 a.m. appointment and both were looking forward to the manicure and pedicure that they had booked. Tate looked after both of them by getting them a cup of coffee and talking with them about how their holidays had been. Building a rapport with customers and looking after customers were main priorities for the salon. Jill felt that if the customers were happy, then the business would mostly look after itself.

QUESTION 1

Why did Jill know that the day was going to be a busy one?

Answer:

QUESTION 2

Why was the salon short-staffed and how many staff members were available?

Answer:

QUESTION 3
What treatment did Caryle carry out first?

Answer:

QUESTION 4
What treatments did Carlene and Rhiannon look forward to having?

Answer:

QUESTION 5
What was one of the main priorities for Jill in looking after her business?

Answer:

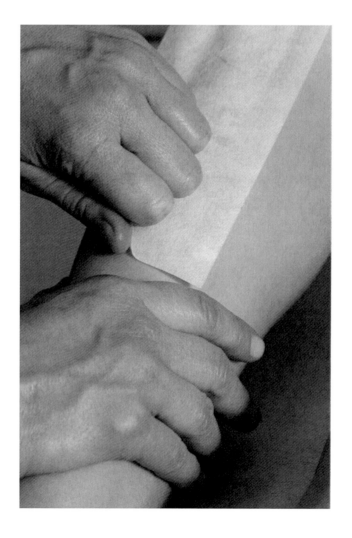

MATHEMATICS

Unit 4: General Mathematics

Short-answer questions

Specific instructions to students

- This unit will help you to improve your general mathematical skills.
- Read the following questions and answer all of them in the spaces provided.
- You may not use a calculator.
- You need to show all working.

QUESTION 1

What unit of measurement would you use to measure:

a   the length of French tips?

Answer:

_____

b   the temperature of steriliser?

Answer:

_____

c   the amount of acrylic liquid?

Answer:

_____

d   the weight of a salon chair?

Answer:

_____

e   the voltage of a nail dryer?

Answer:

_____

f   the length of a body wrap?

Answer:

_____

g   the cost of a treatment?

Answer:

_____

QUESTION 2

Write an example of the following and give an instance where it may be found in the beauty industry:

a   percentages

Answer:

_____

b   decimals

Answer:

_____

c   fractions

Answer:

_____

d   mixed numbers

Answer:

_____

e   ratios

Answer:

_____

f   angles

Answer:

_____

QUESTION 3
Convert the following units:

a   12 kg to grams

Answer:

_____

b   4 t to kilograms

Answer:

_____

c   120 cm to metres

Answer:

_____

d   1140 mL to litres

Answer:

_____

e   1650 g to kilograms

Answer:

_____

f   1880 kg to tonnes

Answer:

_____

g   13 m to centimetres

Answer:

_____

h   4.5 L to millilitres

Answer:

_____

QUESTION 4
Write the following in descending order:

0.4   0.04   4.1   40.0   400.00   4.0

Answer:

_____

QUESTION 5
Write the decimal number that is between the following:

a   0.2 and 0.4

Answer:

_____

b   1.8 and 1.9

Answer:

_____

c   12.4 and 12.5

Answer:

_____

d   28.3 and 28.4

Answer:

_____

e   101.5 and 101.7

Answer:

_____

QUESTION 6
Round off the following numbers to two decimal places:

a   12.346

Answer:

_____

b   2.251

Answer:

_____

c   123.897

Answer:

_____

d 688.882

Answer:

_____

e 1209.741

Answer:

_____

QUESTION 7
Estimate the following by approximation:

a 1288 × 19 =

Answer:

_____

b 201 × 20 =

Answer:

_____

c 497 × 12.2 =

Answer:

_____

d 1008 × 10.3 =

Answer:

_____

e 399 × 22 =

Answer:

_____

f 201 − 19 =

Answer:

_____

g 502 − 61 =

Answer:

_____

h 1003 − 49 =

Answer:

_____

i 10 001 − 199 =

Answer:

_____

j 99.99 − 39.8 =

Answer:

_____

QUESTION 8
What do the following add up to?

a $4, $4.99 and $144.95

Answer:

_____

b 8.75, 6.9 and 12.55

Answer:

_____

c 65 mL, 18 mL and 209 mL

Answer:

_____

d 21.3 g, 119 g and 884.65 g

Answer:

_____

QUESTION 9
Subtract the following:

a 2338 from 7117

Answer:

_____

b 1786 from 3112

Answer:

_____

c 5979 from 8014

Answer:

_____

d 11 989 from 26 221

Answer:

_____

e 108 767 from 231 111

Answer:

QUESTION 10

Use division to solve the following:

a $2177 \div 7 =$

Answer:

---

b $4484 \div 4 =$

Answer:

---

c $63.9 \div 0.3 =$

Answer:

---

d $121.63 \div 1.2 =$

Answer:

---

e $466.88 \div 0.8 =$

Answer:

QUESTION 11

Using BODMAS, solve:

a $(6 \times 9) \times 5 + 7 - 2 =$

Answer:

---

b $(9 \times 8) \times 4 + 6 - 1 =$

Answer:

---

c $3 \times (5 \times 7) + 11 - 8 =$

Answer:

---

d $5 \times (8 \times 3) + 9 - 6 =$

Answer:

---

e $7 + 6 \times 3 + (9 \times 6) - 9 =$

Answer:

---

f $6 + 9 \times 4 + (6 \times 7) - 21 =$

Answer:

The following information is provided for Question 11.

To solve using BODMAS, in order from left to right, solve the Brackets first, then Of, then Division, then Multiplication, then Addition and lastly Subtraction. The following example has been done for your reference.

EXAMPLE :
Solve $(4 \times 7) \times 2 + 6 - 4$.

STEP 1
Solve the Brackets first: $(4 \times 7) = 28$

STEP 2
No Division so next solve Multiplication: $28 \times 2 = 56$

STEP 3
Addition is next: $56 + 6 = 62$

STEP 4
Subtraction is the last process: $62 - 4 = 58$

FINAL ANSWER

58

9780170190763

Unit 5: Basic Operations

Section A: Addition

QUESTION 1

A beauty therapist completes three treatments to three customers before lunch. The treatments include: a standard manicure for $20, a full leg wax for $38 and a deluxe pedicure for $28. What would be the total cost?

Answer:

QUESTION 2

Four customers had the following treatments respectively: a French full set of nails costing $60, an eyelash and eyebrow tint costing $18, a half leg wax costing $120 and a body exfoliation for $50. What is the total?

Answer:

QUESTION 3

A beauty salon stocks 127 gowns, 268 cans of water resistant spray-on tan and 323 various sizes of disposable gloves. How many items in total are in stock?

Answer:

QUESTION 4

The following treatments are completed in the morning: an express pedicure for $35, wedding tips for $45, a bikini wax for $15, a lip and chin wax for $17 and a full body tan for $45. How much money is charged for these treatments in total?

Answer:

QUESTION 5

A beauty therapist takes the following amount of time to complete specific treatments: deluxe manicure – 35 minutes, detoxifying body massage – 45 minutes, a warm body wrap – 75 minutes and a back massage – 30 minutes.

a   How much time has been taken in minutes?

Answer:

b   How much time has been taken in hours and minutes?

Answer:

QUESTION 6

A beauty therapy studio offers the following treatments and prices for a senior high school group preparing for their formal: full leg wax for $25, a deluxe pedicure for $35, an eyelash perm for $45 and a paraffin hand treatment for $25. How much would be spent by a student requiring all four treatments?

Answer:

QUESTION 7

A beauty salon offers several different waxing treatments for clients at the following prices: back wax for $35, ear and nose wax for $15, Brazilian wax for $49, underarm wax for $15, full leg wax for $45 and a full G-string wax for $79. If the therapist completed one of each treatment, what would the total takings be?

Answer:

QUESTION 8

A staff member completes three piercings: two ear piercings on two different clients costing $45 each and a nose piercing, including studs, for $50. Added to each treatment is $8 for the antiseptic healing lotion. How much is charged for all three clients in total?

Answer:

QUESTION 9

One client requires a manicure and the other requires a pedicure. If the beauty salon charges $29 for the manicure and $55 for the pedicure, what will the total come to for both clients?

Answer:

QUESTION 10

A client pays $50, $59 and $49 to have treatments that include: wedding make-up, eyelash perm and tint, and a spray tan, respectively. How much does the total come to?

Answer:

Section B: Subtraction

Short-answer questions

Specific instructions to students

- This section will help you to improve your subtraction skills for basic operations.
- Read the following questions and answer all of them in the spaces provided.
- You may not use a calculator.
- You need to show all working.

QUESTION 1

A salon purchases beauty wax skin care products for $128. How much change is given from $150?

Answer:

QUESTION 2

Four new hair and beauty equipment cases are bought for a total of $135. How much change is given from $200?

Answer:

QUESTION 3

A beauty salon is updating its equipment and purchases five adjustable beauty equipment chairs for a total cost of $1255. How much change is given from $1500?

Answer:

QUESTION 4

A beauty therapist uses 27 nail tips from a box that contains 150 nail tips. How many are left in the box?

Answer:

QUESTION 5

A glycolic exfoliation consisting of six treatments costs $425. The manager takes off a discount of $35.00. How much does the customer need to pay?

Answer:

QUESTION 6

A salon uses 31 cuticle eraser stones from a box that contains 50 cuticle eraser stones. How many are left in the box?

Answer:

9780170190763

QUESTION 7

The following amounts of cuticle oil are used on three clients: 5 mL, 3 mL and 6 mL. How much cuticle oil is left from a bottle that contained 15 mL?

Answer:

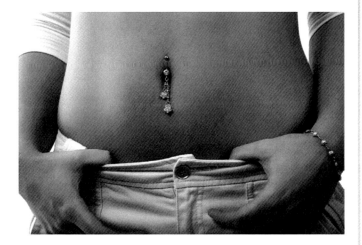

QUESTION 8

Over three months, 74 bellybutton rings are purchased from a beauty stockist. The box initially contained 93 bellybutton rings. How many are now left?

Answer:

QUESTION 9

The overall yearly takings for a major beauty salon is $132 432. The cost of staff wages comes to $78 968. How much of the takings is left after staff wages are paid?

Answer:

QUESTION 10

A bag contains 1400 French tips. If 110 are used over two months, how many remain in the bag?

Answer:

Section C: Multiplication

Short-answer questions

Specific instructions to students

- This section will help you to improve your multiplication skills for basic operations.
- Read the following questions and answer all of them in the spaces provided.
- You may not use a calculator.
- You need to show all working.

QUESTION 1

If one callus remover costs $2, how much would 25 cost?

Answer:

QUESTION 2

If a toe separator costs 55 cents, how much would it cost to purchase 50 for a beauty salon?

Answer:

QUESTION 3

Five clients want a paraffin hand treatment at a beauty salon. The salon charges $17 per client. What are the total takings from the five clients?

Answer:

QUESTION 4

Six customers require a half leg waxing at a cost of $15 each. What are the total takings from the customers?

Answer:

QUESTION 5

A salon charges $29 for a spray tan. What would be the takings if 13 clients had the spray tan treatment?

Answer:

QUESTION 6

A group of seven clients decide to have facials at a beauty salon. The cost of each facial is $45. What are the total takings?

Answer:

QUESTION 7

A busy city salon uses, on average, nine pairs of exfoliating gloves each day. How many pairs would be used over 31 days of a month?

Answer:

QUESTION 8

Each week, a beauty salon uses 27 pedicure files to remove excess skin. How many would be used over a 28-day month?

Answer:

QUESTION 9

Each week, an average of three bottles of natural nail treatment are used to enhance and rejuvenate nails at a salon. How many bottles would be used over a year (52 weeks)?

Answer:

QUESTION 10

A customer purchases seven glass heart charms so that they have one for each day of the week. If each one costs $2, how much will all seven cost?

Answer:

Section D: Division

Short-answer questions

Specific instructions to students

- This section will help you to improve your division skills for basic operations.
- Read the following questions and answer all of them in the spaces provided.
- You may not use a calculator.
- You need to show all working.

QUESTION 1

A beauty salon has 24 customers booked in on a Friday morning. If there are four chairs and four beauty therapists working, how many customers will each therapist attend?

Answer:

QUESTION 2

If a beauty therapist earns $568 (before tax) for working a six-day week, how much would they earn per day?

Answer:

QUESTION 3

A salon manager purchases 60 one-litre bottles of acrylic nail remover. If each box contains 12 bottles, how many boxes are there?

Answer:

QUESTION 4

A salon completes 720 treatments in three months. How many treatments have been completed, on average, per month?

Answer:

9780170190763

QUESTION 5

A beauty therapist uses 180 soft pink pearl tips for each of her clients. How many clients are there, assuming each client has ten fingers?

Answer:

QUESTION 6

One month's takings for a beauty salon are $15 677. How much are the takings per week, on average, for the same salon?

Answer:

QUESTION 7

At a yearly stocktake, a store person at a beauty salon counts 78 pairs of pedi slippers. If they are packed so that there are six pairs in each box, how many boxes would there be?

Answer:

QUESTION 8

A salon orders in 36 12-piece nail art brush sets. If there are six employees, how many sets will each employee get?

Answer:

QUESTION 9

A beauty salon's takings are $8438 over six days. How much, on average, would this be per day?

Answer:

QUESTION 10

A franchise of beauty salons uses 156 bottles of acrylic liquid over a year. How many bottles is that per month?

Answer:

Section A: Addition

QUESTION 1

If four bottles of acrylic sealer are purchased for $75.20 and six bottles of acrylic powder are purchased for $59.70, what is the total for the purchases?

Answer:

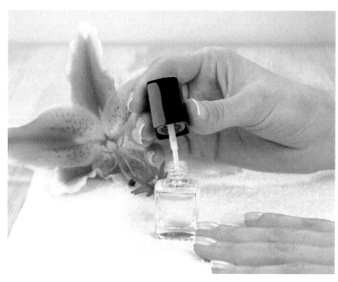

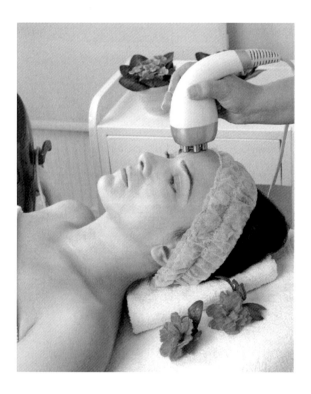

QUESTION 2

A beauty salon purchases airbrushed tips #15 for $22.95, advanced formula resin for $18.95, an ultrasonic skin care unit for $294.55 and a mini paraffin wax heater for $69.50. How much has been spent?

Answer:

QUESTION 3

A mini UV steriliser costing $102.50 and a hot towel cabinet with a UV light costing $53.75 is purchased by a salon manager. What is the total cost?

Answer:

QUESTION 4

A 12-pack of cuticle sticks is purchased for $5.95 and a callus removal kit for $48.50. How much is the total of the purchase?

Answer:

QUESTION 5

A customer purchases the following from a beauty store: a manicure brush for $1.99, two pedicure files for $5.50, 500 mL acrylic liquid for $46.50 and a 100 mL bottle of nail polish remover for $3.95. What is the total?

Answer:

QUESTION 6

The following items are on special and a customer decides to purchase one of each. The items include: nail buffing cream for $5.95, nail primer for $10.75 and hand and skin lotion for $9.50. How much do the purchases total?

Answer:

QUESTION 7

A beauty salon purchases the following items to replace what they have used: blue pearl tips for $14.50, clear full well tips for $2.95, a set of coloured tips for $5.95 and French tips for $13.75. What is the total?

Answer:

QUESTION 8

Three different customers purchase the following: fast dry topcoat for nails costing $10.75, glitter nail polish costing $7.85 and tip blender for $8.50. How much will be the total cost of all three purchases?

Answer:

QUESTION 9

A beauty store sells the following: a bottle of blue nail polish costing $7.85, a 90-piece eye shadow, blush, lipstick and powder set for $31.65, a 15 mL bottle of primer for $10.45, a deluxe French acrylic kit for $59.95 and a pink crystal dangle for $5.75. What is the total in sales?

Answer:

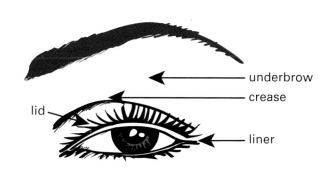

underbrow

crease

lid

liner

QUESTION 10

A beauty salon's daily takings over a six-day week are $889.90, $945.50, $1555.50, $2135.50, $732.50 and $569.25. What is the total of the week's takings at this salon?

Answer:

Section B: Subtraction

Short-answer questions

Specific instructions to students

- This section will help you to improve your subtraction skills when working with decimals.
- Read the following questions and answer all of them in the spaces provided.
- You may not use a calculator.
- You need to show all working.

QUESTION 1

A customer purchases $38.65 worth of beauty products. What change will be given from a $50 note?

Answer:

QUESTION 2

An employee gets paid $568.50 for a week's work. If $78.50 is used to pay bills, $45.75 is paid for petrol and $126 is spent on entertainment, how much money does the employee have left?

Answer:

QUESTION 3

A customer gets a body detox treatment that includes: cleansing, exfoliating, steaming and extraction, and a treatment gel to smooth and rebalance the skin. The cost is $63.50. The customer pays with a $50 and a $20 note. How much change is given?

Answer:

QUESTION 4

A beauty therapist works 38 hours and earns $445.60. She uses $34.75 for petrol and $84.50 for entertainment. How much is left?

Answer:

QUESTION 5

Three customers want a full set of acrylic nails, gel overlay and a manicure, respectively. Each treatment costs $65.50, $53.50 and $27.95. One customer pays for the three treatments with three $50 notes. How much change is given?

Answer:

QUESTION 6

A foot therapy treatment is designed to replenish and repair overexposed feet. The client wanting this treatment is charged $22.50. She pays with two $20 notes. How much change is given?

Answer:

QUESTION 7

The members of a bridal party want to have a 30-minute electrolysis treatment. The total comes to $125.50. What change is given if two $100 notes are used to pay the bill?

Answer:

QUESTION 8

A compressor and airbrush kit are purchased for a salon for $315.50. Six pairs of stainless steel stork scissors are also purchased for a total of $40.80 and five pairs of tweezers, which cost $30.25. The items are paid for from the float in the till which totals $518.55 before the purchases. How much remains in the till after the purchases are paid for?

Answer:

QUESTION 9

A manager buys two glass display hands for displaying nail art and/or jewellery for $36.50, two nail polish dryers for $29.50 and a pack of 50 disposable salon towels for $9.50. If four $20 notes are used to pay the bill, how much change is given?

Answer:

QUESTION 10

A foundation brush costs $24.50, light concealer foundation costs $12.75, eye shadow costs $5.95 and medium foundation concealer costs $11.75 at a beauty salon. If the customer pays for these items with two $50 notes, how much change is given?

Answer:

Section C: Multiplication

QUESTION 1

If one rhinestone carousel costs $15.95, how much will five cost?

Answer:

QUESTION 2

If a salon uses six bottles of French polish costing $9.50 each, how much will all six cost?

Answer:

QUESTION 3

A salon manager purchases six pairs of pedi slippers at a cost of $1.95 each. What is the total?

Answer:

QUESTION 4

An assistant manager purchases eight deluxe acrylic kits that cost $69.95 per kit. How much is the total cost?

Answer:

QUESTION 5

A customer buys two professional acrylic kits valued at $249.95. What is the total?

Answer:

QUESTION 6

Six clients have a facial costing $35.50. What are the total takings from the clients?

Answer:

QUESTION 7

If 13 senior citizens have a diamond microdermabrasion at a cost of $67.50 each, what would be the total takings?

Answer:

QUESTION 8

A bridal party of five all have the three-quarter leg wax treatment costing $30.95 each. How much will the total bill be for all five?

Answer:

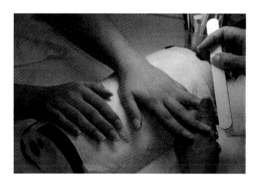

QUESTION 9

A group of seven Year 12 students are preparing for their formal. They all decide to receive the package that includes a standard manicure, standard pedicure, bikini wax, full leg wax and make-up. The cost per student is $125.75. How much will the total bill be for the group?

Answer:

QUESTION 10

Four senior citizens treat themselves to a mini facial. The cost per person is $32.50, which includes a deep cleansing treatment and a relaxing facial without extractions. What is the total bill for the four people?

Answer:

Section D: Division

QUESTION 1

A beauty salon's takings for a six-day week are $3628.55. How much is the daily average takings for the week?

Answer:

QUESTION 2

A salon assistant manager earns $590.60 per five-day working week. How much is earned per day?

Answer:

QUESTION 3

A salon's takings are $5785.50 over five days. How much are the daily average takings?

Answer:

QUESTION 4

A paraffin facial is completed on three customers. The total cost comes to $165.90. How much does each customer pay, if they are charged the same amount?

Answer:

QUESTION 5

Three customers have a full body spray tan at a total cost of $90.90. How much is each customer charged?

Answer:

QUESTION 6

Four customers have a 60-minute aromatherapy full body massage. The total bill comes to $336.80. How much does each customer pay?

Answer:

QUESTION 7

Six customers have a 45-minute, herbal, white-mud purifying back treatment, which comes to a total of $393.60. What is each customer charged?

Answer:

QUESTION 8

A beauty salon completes five eyelash and eyebrow tints for different customers. The total that is charged for all five customers is $93.75. How much is each customer charged?

Answer:

QUESTION 9

Eight customers are charged a total of $96.80 to have a bikini wax. How much is the cost per customer?

Answer:

QUESTION 10

Three customers want a deluxe pedicure that includes their nails cut and filed, feet filed, feet soaked and exfoliated, treatment of their cuticles, a mask applied to both feet, a foot massage and their toenails painted. The total comes to $86.85. How much is each customer charged?

Answer:

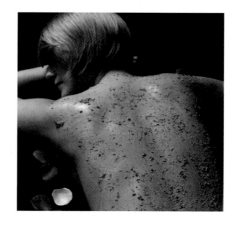

Unit 7: Fractions

Section A: Addition

QUESTION 1

$\frac{1}{2} + \frac{4}{5} =$

Answer:

_____

QUESTION 2

$2\frac{2}{4} + 1\frac{2}{3} =$

Answer:

_____

QUESTION 3

A beauty therapist uses $\frac{1}{4}$ of a bottle of acrylic liquid on one customer and $\frac{1}{3}$ of a bottle of the same liquid on another customer. What is the total amount of acrylic liquid used? Express your answer as a fraction.

Answer:

_____

QUESTION 4

Two bottles of acrylic sealer each have $\frac{1}{3}$ remaining. How much acrylic sealer is there remaining in total? Express your answer as a fraction.

Answer:

_____

QUESTION 5

A tint bowl has $\frac{2}{3}$ of a small bottle of red colour in it. To make a shade of orange another $\frac{1}{4}$ of a small bottle of yellow tint is added. How much colour, in total, is there in the tint bowl? Express your answer as a fraction.

Answer:

_____

Section B: Subtraction

QUESTION 1

$\frac{2}{3} - \frac{1}{4} =$

Answer:

_____

QUESTION 2

$2\frac{2}{3} - 1\frac{1}{4} =$

Answer:

_____

QUESTION 3

A bottle of cuticle oil is $\frac{2}{3}$ full. If $\frac{1}{3}$ is used on a client, how much cuticle oil is left as a fraction?

Answer:

_____

QUESTION 4

A salon manager has $2\frac{1}{2}$ containers of a liquid used to remove acrylic nails. If $1\frac{1}{3}$ is used on two different customers, how much liquid is left as a fraction?

Answer:

_____

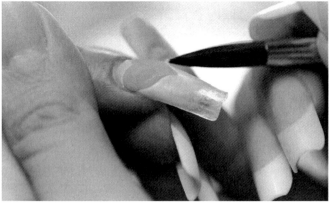

QUESTION 5

A salon has a total of $2\frac{3}{4}$ bottles of non-acetone nail polish remover. If $1\frac{1}{2}$ bottles are used, how much is left as a fraction?

Answer:

_____

Section C: Multiplication

Short-answer questions

Specific instructions to students

- This section is designed to help you to improve your multiplication skills when working with fractions.
- Read the following questions and answer all of them in the spaces provided.
- You may not use a calculator.
- You need to show all working.

QUESTION 1

$\frac{2}{4} \times \frac{2}{3} =$

Answer:

_____

QUESTION 2

$2\frac{2}{3} \times 1\frac{1}{2} =$

Answer:

_____

QUESTION 3

A salon uses two bottles of nail polish that are each $\frac{2}{3}$ full during the day. What is the total amount of nail polish used as a fraction?

Answer:

_____

QUESTION 4

A beauty therapist uses three bottles of primer that are $\frac{3}{4}$ full over a week. How much is used as a fraction?

Answer:

_____

QUESTION 5

A beauty therapist uses four small bottles of lotion that are $\frac{1}{3}$ full over a week. How much is used as a fraction?

Answer:

_____

Section D: Division

Short-answer questions

Specific instructions to students

- This section is designed to help you to improve your division skills when working with fractions.
- Read the following questions and answer all of them in the spaces provided.
- You may not use a calculator.
- You need to show all working.

QUESTION 1

$\frac{2}{3} \div \frac{1}{4} =$

Answer:

QUESTION 2

$2\frac{3}{4} \div 1\frac{1}{3} =$

Answer:

QUESTION 3

A beauty therapist has four empty bottles. Three full bottles of nail polish remover need to be poured into each of the four empty bottles. As a fraction, how much of one bottle of nail polish remover will be in each of the four empty bottles?

Answer:

QUESTON 4

An assistant manager has three empty bottles and two full bottles of hand lotion. He wants to transfer the hand lotion to the empty bottles evenly. As a fraction, how much of a full bottle of hand lotion will be evenly transferred to each of the three empty bottles?

Answer:

QUESTION 5

A beauty therapist wants to begin a manicure for a client but must firstly cleanse the client's hands. Two bottles of hand cream need to be poured into six empty bottles. As a fraction, how much will be poured into each of the six empty bottles from the two full hand cream bottles?

Answer:

Unit 8: Percentages

> **10% rule: Move the decimal one place to the left to get 10%.**

EXAMPLE

10% of $45.00 would be $4.50

QUESTION 1

A bill for make-up for a wedding party comes to $220.00. The customer has a voucher for a 10% discount.

a   How much will the discount be?

Answer:

b   What will the bill come to after the 10% is deducted?

Answer:

QUESTION 2

A customer has a customised 60-minute facial, a 30-minute massage, full leg waxing, underarm waxing and a bikini wax. In addition, she decides to have a spray tan and a manicure. The total cost comes to $225.00. A '10% off' voucher is used to reduce the final cost.

a   How much will the discount be?

Answer:

b   How much is the final bill?

Answer:

QUESTION 3

A beauty salon purchases five 90-piece eye shadow, blush, lipstick and powder sets at a cost of $167.50. The salon is given a 10% discount on the purchase.

a   How much will the discount be?

Answer:

b   What is the final cost?

Answer:

QUESTION 4

A salon manager buys six deluxe acrylic kits for a total wholesale price of $359.70. A 5% discount is given.

a   How much is the discount worth?

Answer:

b   How much is paid? (Hint: Find 10%, halve it, then subtract it from the overall price.)

Answer:

QUESTION 5

A beauty therapist purchases two compressor and airbrush kits at $620, a spare airbrush for $63 and four foundation brushes for $120.

a   How much is the total?

Answer:

b   How much would a 20% discount be?

Answer:

c   What is the final cost after discount?

Answer:

QUESTION 6

The following items are purchased for a beauty salon:
24 10 g sifter pots of eye shadow for $162, 15 sets of
4 mm coloured-glass heart dangles for $187.50,
12 foundation brushes for $312, two nail polish dryers
for $32 and four rhinestone carousels for $56.

a   What is the total of these items?

Answer:

_____

b   What would a 10% discount be?

Answer:

_____

c   What is the final cost after the discount?

Answer:

_____

QUESTION 7

A store offers 20% off the price of any beauty product as
long as the customer spends at least $100. If a customer
spends $105, how much would a collection of six bottles
of glitter nail polish, normally priced at $39, cost?

Answer:

_____

QUESTION 8

A particular range of beauty products are discounted by
15%. If the recommended retail price of six bottles of tip
blender is $48, how much will the discount be?

Answer:

_____

QUESTION 9

A brand of hand lotion is priced at $16.90 as per the
recommended retail price. The store has a '20% sale' on
this item. How much will the hand lotion cost during
the sale?

Answer:

_____

QUESTION 10

Several styles of dangle charms are priced at $5.90 each.
During a sale, the charms are sold at 30% off. What will
the selling price be after the discount?

Answer:

_____

Unit 9: Measurement Conversions

Short-answer questions

Specific instructions to students

- This unit is designed to help you to improve your skills and increase your speed in converting one measurement into another.
- Read the following questions and answer all of them in the spaces provided.
- You may not use a calculator.
- You need to show all working.

QUESTION 1

How many millimetres are there in 1 cm?

Answer:

QUESTION 2

How many centimetres are there in 1 m?

Answer:

QUESTION 3

How many millimetres are there in 1 m?

Answer:

QUESTION 4

If a beauty therapist uses two brush strokes every 2 cm, how many brush strokes would there be in 10 cm?

Answer:

QUESTION 5

How many millilitres are there in a 1.5 L bottle of hand lotion?

Answer:

QUESTION 6

How many litres does 3500 mL of spray tan make?

Answer:

QUESTION 7

A beauty salon's chair weighs a quarter of a tonne. How many kilograms is that?

Answer:

QUESTION 8

A delivery truck weighs 2 t. How many kilograms is that?

Answer:

QUESTION 9

A make-up product delivery truck weighs 4750 kg. How many tonnes is that?

Answer:

QUESTION 10

A beauty salon's floor measures 4.8 m wide and 12 m long. How far is it around the perimeter of the salon?

Answer:

From time to time, it will be important to be able to convert inches to centimetres.

Remember: 1 inch = 2.54 cm (you can round this down to 2.5 cm if you wish)

QUESTION 11

Brian needed to trim his client's nails before applying nail polish to the nails. If the nails measured 2 inches, how long would they be in centimetres?

Answer:

9780170190763

QUESTION 12

On Tuesday, Pauline had two customers who wanted soft pink pearl tips. One customer wanted them 3 inches long, the other wanted 4-inch tips. What length is each of these tips in centimetres?

Answer:

QUESTION 13

Jane is going to the end-of-year formal and she wants a 3-inch long glass heart charm. How long will this be in centimetres?

Answer:

QUESTION 14

Kev was working on a glass display hand model and wanted to see what 5-inch nails would look like. How long would the nails be in centimetres?

Answer:

QUESTION 15

Paula loved having long nails and decided to get three and a half inch clear full well tips. How long would the tips be in centimetres?

Answer:

QUESTION 16

Maiye wanted 5 cm white tips. How long would these be in inches? (Hint: divide 25 by 2.5)

Answer:

QUESTION 17

A beauty therapist worked on a hand model and added natural tips that were 10 cm long. How long would these tips be in inches?

Answer:

QUESTION 18

Kalyan is getting married on Saturday. She wants to have a leg wax that will be 50 cm long, up her leg. How long is this in inches?

Answer:

QUESTION 19

Chris wants his nails to be long. He chooses to get fancy tips that are trimmed to 12.5 cm. What length is this in inches?

Answer:

QUESTION 20

After receiving a pedicure, Lucy asks for 2.5 cm clear tips for her feet. How long is this in inches?

Answer:

Short-answer questions

Specific instructions to students

- This unit will help you to calculate how much a job is worth and how long you need to complete the job.
- Read the following questions and answer all of them in the spaces provided.
- You may not use a calculator.
- You need to show all working.

QUESTION 1

Briony earns $360.60 net (take home per week). How much does Briony earn per year (52 weeks) if this is her regular weekly salary?

Answer:

QUESTION 2

Christie starts work at 8.00 a.m. and has a break at 10.30 a.m. for 20 minutes. Lunch starts at 12.30 p.m. and finishes at 1.30 p.m. Christie then works through to 4.00 p.m.

a   How long are the breaks in total, in minutes?

Answer:

b   How many hours and minutes have been worked in total, excluding breaks?

Answer:

QUESTION 3

Lorna earns $12.50 an hour and works a 38-hour week. How much are her gross earnings (before tax)?

Answer:

QUESTION 4

Melissa gets paid $411 net for her week's work. From this, she spends money on a brush kit for $36.95, jewellery worth $19.55, entertainment for $95, CDs worth $59.97 and a callus remover that costs $12.60.

a   What is the total of all money spent?

Answer:

b   How much is left?

Answer:

QUESTION 5

Several customers enter a beauty salon at the same time. The staff takes the following amount of time for each customer respectively: 34 minutes, 18 minutes, 7 minutes, 44 minutes and 59 minutes. How much time, in minutes and hours, has been spent on these customers in total?

Answer:

QUESTION 6

A customer requires a full body wrap. This takes the beauty therapist $1\frac{1}{4}$ hours to complete.

a   How many minutes is this?

Answer:

b   How many hours are left, if the beauty therapist normally works an 8-hour day?

Answer:

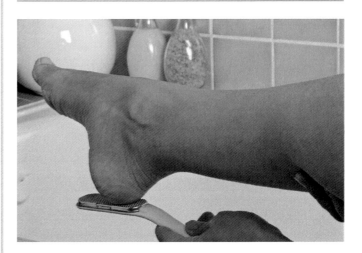

QUESTION 7

A client wants a pedicure that includes nails cut and filed, feet filed, feet soaked and exfoliated, cuticles treated, foot massage and, finally, toenails painted. This takes $1\frac{1}{2}$ hours to complete. Another client wants a manicure that includes cutting and shaping of the nails, cuticles treated, hands exfoliated, a hand massage, hands dipped in paraffin wax and nails painted. This takes $1\frac{1}{4}$ hours.

a   How many hours and part-hours were spent on the two clients? State your answer as a fraction.

Answer:

_____

b   If the beauty therapist works an 8-hour day, how many hours are there left to work in the day, including breaks?

Answer:

_____

QUESTION 8

A beauty salon charges $125 for a natural, pure-clay nourishing full body treatment. This takes the beauty therapist 1 hour and 50 minutes to complete.

a   In hours and minutes, how long will be left in a 8-hour working day?

Answer:

_____

b   How many minutes will the treatment take?

Answer:

_____

QUESTION 9

A salon manager begins work at 7.00 a.m. and works until 4.00 p.m. There is a morning break for 20 minutes, a lunch break for 60 minutes and an afternoon break of 20 minutes.

a   How much time has been spent on breaks?

Answer:

_____

b   How much time has been spent working?

Answer:

_____

QUESTION 10

A beauty salon's takings for the day come to $1850.50. The salon manager was the only staff member available to work that day. If she spent 10 hours at the salon, how much would be the hourly rate, on average?

Answer:

_____

Unit 11: Squaring Numbers

Section A: Introducing square numbers

Short-answer questions

Specific instructions to students

- This section is designed to help you to improve your skills and increase your speed in squaring numbers.
- Read the following questions and answer all of them in the spaces provided.
- You may not use a calculator.
- You need to show all working.

> Any number squared is multiplied by itself.

EXAMPLE

4 squared $= 4^2 = 4 \times 4 = 16$

QUESTION 1

$6^2 =$

Answer:

QUESTION 2

$8^2 =$

Answer:

QUESTION 3

$12^2 =$

Answer:

QUESTION 4

$3^2 =$

Answer:

QUESTION 5

$7^2 =$

Answer:

QUESTION 6

$11^2 =$

Answer:

QUESTION 7

$10^2 =$

Answer:

QUESTION 8

$9^2 =$

Answer:

QUESTION 9

$2^2 =$

Answer:

QUESTION 10

$4^2 =$

Answer:

9780170190763

Section B: Applying square numbers to the trade

Worded practical problems

Specific instructions to students

- This section is designed to help you to improve your skills and increase your speed in calculating volumes of rectangular or square objects. The worded questions make the content relevant to everyday situations.
- Read the following questions and answer all of them in the spaces provided.
- You may not use a calculator.
- You need to show all working.

QUESTION 1

If there are 5 × 5 professional fast-dry topcoat bottles in a box, how many bottles are there in total?

Answer:

QUESTION 2

Glitter nail polish bottles are delivered to a beauty salon stacked 6 × 6. What is the total number of bottles?

Answer:

QUESTION 3

There are 12 × 12 foundation brushes packed into a box. How many are in the box?

Answer:

QUESTION 4

A warehouse floor has an area that is 15 m × 15 m. How much floor area is this in square metres (m²)?

Answer:

QUESTION 5

A merchandise box contains opal glitter nail polish that are in rows of 8 × 8. How many containers of the product are there?

Answer:

QUESTION 6

A salon manager unpacks two boxes to put on display. The first box contains 4 × 4 100 g pots of acrylic powder. The second box contains purple glitter nail polish that are packed in a 3 × 3 formation. How many stock items are there in total?

Answer:

QUESTION 7

A box of clear gel bottles arrive at a beauty salon. If they are packed in a 20 × 20 formation, how many are there?

Answer:

QUESTION 8

A salon stocks the following: 5 × 5 gel brushes, 3 × 3 100 mL cleanser bottles and 10 × 10 French white tips. How many items of stock are there in total?

Answer:

QUESTION 9

The following items are stocked by a beauty salon:
5×5 bottles of cuticle oil, 5×5 pink gel tips and
5×5 cuticle nippers. How many items are there in total?

Answer:

QUESTION 10

A complete gel kit consists of the following items:
3×3 foam files, 2×2 gel brushes, 2×2 primer and
3×3 white gel. How many items are there in total?

Answer:

Unit 12: Vouchers

QUESTION 1

A customer books in for a course of five treatments and receives the sixth for free. The customer knows that they need to prepay and the total comes to $350. The customer has a voucher for 20% off.

a   How much is taken off because of the voucher?

Answer:

b   How much is the final cost?

Answer:

QUESTION 2

A client books a treatment and rebooks for another treatment at a later date. The client receives 10% off the next treatment.

a   If the next treatment costs $275, how much is the discount?

Answer:

b   How much will the rebooked treatment cost?

Answer:

QUESTION 3

A beauty salon charges $45.50 for the first treatment for a 30-minute manicure. Each manicure treatment after the first is charged at $37.

a   If the client has three manicures over the year, how much will they be charged?

Answer:

b   If they have a '10% off' voucher that they can use, how much will they be charged for the three manicures after using the voucher?

Answer:

QUESTION 4

A customer wants a 30-minute multivitamin hand-and-foot treatment for which the salon charges $55. The customer has a '30% off' voucher.

a   How much will the voucher take off?

Answer:

b   What will be the final cost?

Answer:

QUESTION 5

A bridal party of five book into a salon and want the following treatments: reflex foot therapy costing $72, a 20-minute revitalising foot treatment costing $43, a one-hour deluxe spa pedicure for $68, a buff and polish for $28.50 and a 45-minute deluxe manicure for $55.50.

a   What is the total for all treatments?

Answer:

b   The bridal party has a '15% off' voucher. By how much is the final bill reduced due to the voucher?

Answer:

c   What is the final bill for all five clients?

Answer:

QUESTION 6

A day-package gift voucher from a beauty salon is given as a present. The day package includes waxing, tanning, eyelash tinting, body wrap, exfoliation, covered-in gel, algae or mud, scalp treatment, a Dermalogica face-mapping facial (including an eyebrow wax), pedicure in a spa, spray tan and application of make-up. The cost of the day package is $445. A 15% voucher is included as a one-off special for Christmas.

a   How much is the discount, using the voucher?

Answer:

b   What is the final cost?

Answer:

QUESTION 7

A salon offers day packages for $228 which include a manicure and hand massage, a facial that helps to clean, relax and rejuvenate the skin, a back and leg massage and a pedicure that includes a foot massage. A '25% off' voucher is used.

a   How much will the voucher take off the cost?

Answer:

b   What is the final cost?

Answer:

QUESTION 8

A package for men is offered by a salon. It comprises a skin care treatment for men, including a facial where the face is cleansed and exfoliated, and a deep tissue face massage. An eyebrow wax is optional and the treatment is completed with a buff and file of the nails. The price is $121.50. A '10% off' voucher is used.

a   How much will the voucher take off the cost?

Answer:

b   What is the final cost?

Answer:

QUESTION 9

Three clients have a '15% off' voucher and they require three different treatments. The first client wants a multivitamin treatment that acts as a vitamin repair and hydroxy acid exfoliation. This is most important for prematurely aging skin and it aims to improve the elasticity of the skin, add to the tone and develop texture. The 30-minute treatment costs $64. The second client wants a 60-minute medicated cleaning treatment that purifies and cleanses skin, followed by extractions. The cost is $102. The third customer wants a skin renewal peel that takes 45 minutes and includes a mask and peel, removal of dead skin cells and smoothes out facial lines and wrinkles. The cost is $77.

a   How much is the total cost for all three customers without the voucher?

Answer:

b   How much will the voucher take off the cost?

Answer:

c   What is the final cost for all three customers?

Answer:

QUESTION 10

Six Year 12 students book in for treatments leading up to their formal. The six treatments are a scalp treatment for $62, a 30-minute multivitamin hand-and-foot treatment for $55, a 30-minute eye contour treatment for $47, eyebrow wax for $25, lip bleach for $17 and a Brazilian wax and shape for $68. The students have a voucher for 10% off.

a   How much will the total be before using the voucher?

Answer:

b   How much will the voucher take off?

Answer:

c   What is the final cost for all six students?

Answer:

9780170190763

Unit 13: Deals

QUESTION 1

A shop sells lipstick for $8.50 each or two for $16.

a   Which is the better deal and why?

Answer:

_____

b   How much is the price difference per bottle?

Answer:

_____

QUESTION 2

A store sells a spangle carousel for $12.95 each or two for $25.

a   Which is the better buy?

Answer:

_____

_____

b   How much is the difference per carousel?

Answer:

_____

QUESTION 3

A cosmetics store has an offer for customers to buy one packet of pearl tips for $14.50 or buy three packets for $39.

a   Which is the better deal?

Answer:

_____

b   How much is the difference?

Answer:

_____

QUESTION 4

A store has soaker bowls that can take acetone for sale at $3.50 each or four for $12.80. Which is the better buy and why?

Answer:

_____

_____

QUESTION 5

A manager wants to buy airbrush paint for the salon. One wholesaler sells the paint for $11.50 each. Another wholesaler sells the same paint in lots of 12 for $120. Which is the better deal and why?

Answer:

_____

_____

QUESTION 6

A shop has an offer where a customer gets a free set of six glitter nail polish worth $35, if they spend over $100. Another shop offers two free sets of glitter nail polish if the customer spends over $150. Which shop would you spend your money in and why?

Answer:

_____

_____

_____

_____

QUESTION 7

A store has a special where if a customer spends $50 they will receive a $10 voucher to purchase more goods at the same store. If a customer spends $200, how much money in vouchers could they expect to receive?

Answer:

_____

QUESTION 8

A store offers a special where if a customer spends $100 they will receive a $15 voucher. A customer purchases $300 worth of goods. How much money in vouchers could they expect to receive?

Answer:

_____

QUESTION 9

A salon offers $20, $50 and $100 gift vouchers. The salon adds $3, $5 and $10 to the price of each voucher respectively when purchased. If a customer purchases one of each voucher, how much will the total cost be?

Answer:

_____

QUESTION 10

If a customer purchases two foundation brushes for $50, they will get a third foundation brush for free. The customer decides to purchase six foundation brushes. How many foundation brushes will the customer end up with, considering the offer?

Answer:

_____

9780170190763

Beauty Therapy
Practice Written Exam
for the Beauty Therapy Trade

Reading time: 10 minutes

Writing time: 1 hour 30 minutes

Section A: Literacy

Section B: General Mathematics

Section C: Trade Mathematics

QUESTION and ANSWER BOOK

Section	Topic	Number of questions	Marks
A	Literacy	7	23
B	General Mathematics	11	25
C	Trade Mathematics	32	52
		Total 50	Total 100

The sections may be completed in the order of your choice.

NO CALCULATORS are to be used during the exam.

Spelling

Read the passage below and then underline the 20 spelling errors.

10 marks

Maria and Amber entered a beauty salon and desided to have diferent treatmentss. They both had been shoping all day and they thought that it was time to spoill themselves. Maria bought an acrylic nail kit while Amber perchased a range of glitter nail colours. Maria decided on a menacure and Amber settled on having a soothing facial. Normaly, the beauty salon would have been very bussy at this time of the day, but the girls were lucky that there had been only a few bokings when they called in. Maria and Amber were happy to have a break from the hussle and bustle of the shopping crowd.

A cape was plased over Amber as the beauty therapist began to prapare her for the facial. All of the equiptment had been sterilised and the beauty therapist explaned to Amber that the treatment would take 30 minates. Meenwhile, Maria was being treated to a manicure and was enjoying a lovely convasation about what she was doing on the weekend. Maria had also decided that she wanted a pedicure and the beauty therapist agread that this would make her feet feel and look great. Everything went according to plan and the results turned out to be wonderfull. Both Maria and Amber had enjoyed their visit to the salon and each felt much better after their treatments.

Correct the spelling errors by writing them out with the correct spelling below.

_____

_____

Alphabetising

Put the following words into alphabetical order.

7 marks

piercing	exfoliation
customer service	eyelash
spray tan	French tips
acrylic nails	manicure
wedding make-up	half leg wax
extraction	body wrap
dangles	lash and brow

_____

_____

_____

_____
_____
_____
_____
_____
_____
_____
_____
_____
_____
_____

Comprehension

Short-answer questions

Specific instructions to students

- Read the following passage and answer the questions on the following page.

Steven and Dorothy started work at the beauty salon at 9.00 a.m. on a Saturday. There were many bookings and they both knew it was going to be a long day as they had been very busy the day before and they were tired. Saturdays were always booked solid as customers often had functions to attend that evening. Steven felt that this could be one of their busiest working days. He decided to ring Sue and ask her to help out. Sue was unavailable as she was going away for the weekend to attend a wedding. Luckily, another beautician, Katie, was available and came into the beauty salon, arriving at 9.25 a.m. Steven's first customer was a woman who wanted a pedicure. Dorothy's first customer was a younger woman who had always wanted a bellybutton piercing but was too shy to get one, until now. Katie's first customer arrived 15 minutes later and this customer wanted a full leg wax.

Everything had been moving along smoothly and Steven had completed three manicures and one pedicure. Dorothy had been kept busy with several customers wanting piercings, as well as one customer wanting a facial. Katie had completed three leg waxes and two facial treatments. Steven took his lunch break and met with his friend Gary, to show him how his hair looked after it had been bleached. Dorothy took her break next and went shopping for designer clothes. Katie met with her partner, Josh, at a café not far from the salon, where they had lunch together. The breaks were staggered, as there needed to be at least two beauty therapists in the salon to tend to customers. By the close of trading, the takings had equalled their best-ever day's takings. Steven, Dorothy and Katie all went to the wine bar next door and enjoyed a well-earned drink.

QUESTION 1   1 mark

Why did Steven and Dorothy feel that it was going to be a long day?

Answer:

_____

_____

_____

QUESTION 2   1 mark

Why were bookings always 'solid' on Saturdays?

Answer:

_____

_____

QUESTION 3   1 mark

What did each beauty therapist's first customer want as their treatment?

Answer:

_____

_____

_____

_____

QUESTION 4   1 mark

What did each person do on his or her break?

Answer:

_____

_____

_____

QUESTION 5   2 marks

Why did the breaks need to be staggered?

Answer:

_____

_____

Section B: General Mathematics

QUESTION 1   1 + 1 + 1 = 3 marks

What unit of measurement would you use to measure:

a the length of acrylic nails

Answer:

_____

b the temperature of a steriliser

Answer:

_____

c the amount of cuticle oil

Answer:

_____

QUESTION 2   1 + 1 + 1 = 3 marks

Write an example of the following and give an instance where it may be found in the beauty therapy industry:

a percentages

Answer:

_____

b decimals

Answer:

_____

c fractions

Answer:

_____

QUESTION 3   1 + 1 = 2 marks

Convert the following units:

a 1 kg to grams

Answer:

_____

b 1500 g to kilograms

Answer:

_____

QUESTION 4 — 1 mark

Write the following in descending order:

0.7   0.71   7.1   70.1   701.00   7.0

Answer:

QUESTION 5 — 1 + 1 = 2 marks

Write the decimal number that is between the following:

a   0.1 and 0.2

Answer:

b   1.3 and 1.4

Answer:

QUESTION 6 — 1 + 1 = 2 marks

Round off the following numbers to two decimal places:

a   5.177

Answer:

b   12.655

Answer:

QUESTION 7 — 1 + 1 = 2 marks

Estimate the following by approximation:

a $101 \times 81 =$

Answer:

b $399 \times 21 =$

Answer:

QUESTION 8 — 1 + 1 = 2 marks

What do the following add up to?

a $25, $13.50 and $165.50

Answer:

b $4, $5.99 and $229.50

Answer:

QUESTION 9 — 1 + 1 = 2 marks

Subtract the following:

a   196 from 813

Answer:

b   5556 from 9223

Answer:

QUESTION 10 — 1 + 1 = 2 marks

Use division to solve:

a $4824 \div 3 =$

Answer:

b $84.2 \div 0.4 =$

Answer:

QUESTION 11 — 2 + 2 = 4 marks

Using BODMAS, solve:

a $(3 \times 7) \times 4 + 9 - 5 =$

Answer:

b $(8 \times 12) \times 2 + 8 - 4 =$

Answer:

Section C: Trade Mathematics

Basic Operations

Addition

QUESTION 1   1 mark

A beauty salon purchases 36 bottles of glitter nail polish, 144 dangles and 15 foundation brushes. How many items have been purchased in total?

Answer:

QUESTION 2   1 mark

Three treatments are completed and each costs $25, $45 and $17. How much has been charged in total?

Answer:

Subtraction

QUESTION 1   1 mark

A salon uses 57 nail tips from a box that contains 150 nail tips. How many remain?

Answer:

QUESTION 2   1 mark

A customer purchases skin care products and the total comes to $124. The manager takes off a discount of $35 during a sale. How much does the customer pay?

Answer:

Multiplication

QUESTION 1   1 mark

A salon completes the following treatments during a day: six deluxe pedicures costing $34 each, two half leg waxes for $35 each and four facials charged at $38 each. What is the total cost?

Answer:

QUESTION 2   1 mark

Seven bottles of cuticle oil are used over the course of one day. If one bottle costs $8, how much will seven bottles cost?

Answer:

Division

QUESTION 1   1 mark

The week's takings for a beauty salon are $5578. If the salon was open for six days, what would the average takings be per day?

Answer:

QUESTION 2   1 mark

At a yearly stocktake at a salon, a store person counts 72 bottles of nail polish remover. If 12 bottles are packed into each box, how many boxes are there?

Answer:

Decimals

Addition

QUESTION 1   1 mark

A customer buys the following products from a store: a can of hair spray for $19.95, a bottle of cuticle oil for $9.50 and a foundation brush for $24.50. How much for the purchases in total?

Answer:

QUESTION 2   1 mark

A store sells the following products during a Christmas sale: tip blender for $7.95; UV topcoat for $11.50 and nail polish dryers for $12.85. How much is the total for all three?

Answer:

Subtraction

QUESTION 1   1 mark

A beauty therapist earns $418.50 per week. From these earnings, $35.95 is spent on clothes and $25.50 is spent on food. How much is left?

Answer:

_____

QUESTION 2   1 mark

A manager purchases two deluxe acrylic kits for $121.50. If they are to be paid for with three $50 notes from the float, how much change will be given?

Answer:

_____

Multiplication

QUESTION 1   1 + 1 = 2 marks

A customer buys three bottles of 15 mL nail primer valued at $12.95 each.

a   How much does it cost for the three bottles?

Answer:

_____

b   What change will be given from $50.00?

Answer:

_____

QUESTION 2   1 + 1 = 2 marks

A customer purchases four $25 gift vouchers at a cost of $28.50 each.

a   What is the total cost of the purchase?

Answer:

_____

b   What change will be given from $120.00?

Answer:

_____

Division

QUESTION 1   2 marks

The daily takings from a beauty salon are $987.00 over five hours during a Saturday morning's trading. How much does this work out to be, on average, per hour?

Answer:

_____

QUESTION 2   2 marks

Four people have full leg waxing. The total for all four customers comes to $88.80. What is the cost to each customer who had the treatment?

Answer:

_____

Fractions

QUESTION 1   2 marks

$\frac{1}{4} + \frac{1}{2} =$

Answer:

_____

QUESTION 2   2 marks

$\frac{4}{5} - \frac{1}{3} =$

Answer:

_____

QUESTION 3   2 marks

$\frac{2}{3} \times \frac{1}{4} =$

Answer:

_____

QUESTION 4   2 marks

$\frac{3}{4} \div \frac{1}{2} =$

Answer:

_____

Percentages

QUESTION 1   2 marks

A salon has a '10% off' sale on all items. If a customer purchases items totalling $149.00, what is the final sale price?

Answer:

_____

QUESTION 2   2 marks

Beauty products are discounted by 20% in a store. If the regular retail price of certain skin products comes to $120.00, how much will the customer pay after the discount?

Answer:

Measurement Conversions

QUESTION 1   2 marks

How many grams are there in 1.85 kg?

Answer:

QUESTION 2   2 marks

35 mm converts to how many centimetres?

Answer:

Earning Wages

QUESTION 1   2 marks

A part-time beautician gets paid $12.50 per hour. If she works 15 hours a week, how much will her gross pay be?

Answer:

QUESTION 2   1 + 1 = 2 marks

A beauty therapist spends the following time on five different customers, receiving five different treatments: 17 minutes, 35 minutes, 19 minutes, 48 minutes and 58 minutes respectively.

a   How much time, in minutes, has been taken?

Answer:

b   How much time, in hours and minutes, has been taken?

Answer:

Squaring Numbers

QUESTION 1   2 marks

What is 7^2?

Answer:

QUESTION 2   2 marks

The floor area of a warehouse measures 13 m × 13 m. What is the total floor area?

Answer:

Vouchers

QUESTION 1   2 marks

A customer purchases beauty products from a salon using a '20% off' voucher. If $148.60 worth of beauty products are purchased, what will be the final cost to the customer once the voucher is used?

Answer:

QUESTION 2   2 marks

A customer purchases goods to the total of $134.60. A voucher for '15% off' is used. How much is charged after the voucher is used?

Answer:

Deals

QUESTION 1   2 marks

A wholesaler has 9 Watt UV lamps on sale for $38.95, or you can buy two for $70. Which is the better deal and how much, if any, will be saved?

Answer:

QUESTION 2   2 marks

A store sells 100 mL acrylic liquid for $12.50 per bottle or three for $35. Which is the better deal and how much, if any, will be saved?

Answer:

Glossary

Acrylic liquid   Gives shine to finished nails. Comes in a non-yellowing format.

Acrylic powder   Can improve flexibility and strength in nails. Great finishing product.

Cuticle oil   Enhances overall nail health and can improve the finished appearance of a manicure.

Dangle   Can include large earrings and/or jewellery features for bellybutton piercings.

Exfoliation   The removal of dead skin cells, either physically by means of abrasive ingredients or implements (e.g. scrubs, cleansing pads), or chemically using enzymes or acids (e.g. alpha and beta hydroxy acids, retinoids).

Extraction   In skin care, this term is used to describe the process of manually removing blackheads, or comedones, from the skin.

Manicure   A cosmetic beauty treatment for the fingernails and hands performed either at home or in a nail salon by a licensed professional nail technician or manicurist. A manicure treatment is not only a treatment for the natural nails but also for the hands. A manicure consists of filing, shaping of the free edge, cuticle treatments, massage of the hand and the application of polish.

Pedicure   A way to improve the appearance of the feet and toenails. It provides a similar service to a manicure.

Piercing   The practice of puncturing or cutting a part of the human body, creating an opening in which jewellery may be worn.

Spray tan   Sunless tanning, self-tanning, fake tanning, or UV-free tanning refers to applying chemicals to the body to produce an effect similar in appearance to a more traditional suntan.

Waxing   A method of semi-permanent hair removal that removes the hair from the root. New hairs will not grow back in the previously waxed area for two to eight weeks. Almost any area of the body can be waxed, including eyebrows, face, bikini area, legs, arms, back, abdomen and feet. There are many types of waxing suitable for removing unwanted hair.

Formulae and Data

Circumference of a Circle

$C = \pi \times d$

where: C = circumference, π = 3.14, d = diameter

Diameter of a Circle

$d = \dfrac{C}{\pi}$

Where: C = circumference, π = 3.14, d = diameter

Area

$A = l \times b$

Area = length × breadth and is given in square units

Volume of a Cube

$V = l \times w \times h$

Volume = length × width × height and is given in cubic units

Volume of a Cylinder

$V_c = \pi \times r^2 \times h$

Where: V_c = volume of a cylinder, π = 3.14, r = radius, h = height

Times Tables

1

1	× 1	=	1
2	× 1	=	2
3	× 1	=	3
4	× 1	=	4
5	× 1	=	5
6	× 1	=	6
7	× 1	=	7
8	× 1	=	8
9	× 1	=	9
10	× 1	=	10
11	× 1	=	11
12	× 1	=	12

2

1	× 2	=	2
2	× 2	=	4
3	× 2	=	6
4	× 2	=	8
5	× 2	=	10
6	× 2	=	12
7	× 2	=	14
8	× 2	=	16
9	× 2	=	18
10	× 2	=	20
11	× 2	=	22
12	× 2	=	24

3

1	× 3	=	3
2	× 3	=	6
3	× 3	=	9
4	× 3	=	12
5	× 3	=	15
6	× 3	=	18
7	× 3	=	21
8	× 3	=	24
9	× 3	=	27
10	× 3	=	30
11	× 3	=	33
12	× 3	=	36

4

1	× 4	=	4
2	× 4	=	8
3	× 4	=	12
4	× 4	=	16
5	× 4	=	20
6	× 4	=	24
7	× 4	=	28
8	× 4	=	32
9	× 4	=	36
10	× 4	=	40
11	× 4	=	44
12	× 4	=	48

5

1	× 5	=	5
2	× 5	=	10
3	× 5	=	15
4	× 5	=	20
5	× 5	=	25
6	× 5	=	30
7	× 5	=	35
8	× 5	=	40
9	× 5	=	45
10	× 5	=	50
11	× 5	=	55
12	× 5	=	60

6

1	× 6	=	6
2	× 6	=	12
3	× 6	=	18
4	× 6	=	24
5	× 6	=	30
6	× 6	=	36
7	× 6	=	42
8	× 6	=	48
9	× 6	=	54
10	× 6	=	60
11	× 6	=	66
12	× 6	=	72

7

1	× 7	=	7
2	× 7	=	14
3	× 7	=	21
4	× 7	=	28
5	× 7	=	35
6	× 7	=	42
7	× 7	=	49
8	× 7	=	56
9	× 7	=	63
10	× 7	=	70
11	× 7	=	77
12	× 7	=	84

8

1	× 8	=	8
2	× 8	=	16
3	× 8	=	24
4	× 8	=	32
5	× 8	=	40
6	× 8	=	48
7	× 8	=	56
8	× 8	=	64
9	× 8	=	72
10	× 8	=	80
11	× 8	=	88
12	× 8	=	96

9

1	× 9	=	9
2	× 9	=	18
3	× 9	=	27
4	× 9	=	36
5	× 9	=	45
6	× 9	=	54
7	× 9	=	63
8	× 9	=	72
9	× 9	=	81
10	× 9	=	90
11	× 9	=	99
12	× 9	=	108

10

1	× 10	=	10
2	× 10	=	20
3	× 10	=	30
4	× 10	=	40
5	× 10	=	50
6	× 10	=	60
7	× 10	=	70
8	× 10	=	80
9	× 10	=	90
10	× 10	=	100
11	× 10	=	110
12	× 10	=	120

11

1	× 11	=	11
2	× 11	=	22
3	× 11	=	33
4	× 11	=	44
5	× 11	=	55
6	× 11	=	66
7	× 11	=	77
8	× 11	=	88
9	× 11	=	99
10	× 11	=	110
11	× 11	=	121
12	× 11	=	132

12

1	× 12	=	12
2	× 12	=	24
3	× 12	=	36
4	× 12	=	48
5	× 12	=	60
6	× 12	=	72
7	× 12	=	84
8	× 12	=	96
9	× 12	=	108
10	× 12	=	120
11	× 12	=	132
12	× 12	=	144

Multiplication Grid

	1	2	3	4	5	6	7	8	9	10	11	12
1	1	2	3	4	5	6	7	8	9	10	11	12
2	2	4	6	8	10	12	14	16	18	20	22	24
3	3	6	9	12	15	18	21	24	27	30	33	36
4	4	8	12	16	20	24	28	32	36	40	44	48
5	5	10	15	20	25	30	35	40	45	50	55	60
6	6	12	18	24	30	36	42	48	54	60	66	72
7	7	14	21	28	35	42	49	56	63	70	77	84
8	8	16	24	32	40	48	56	64	72	80	88	96
9	9	18	27	36	45	54	63	72	81	90	99	108
10	10	20	30	40	50	60	70	80	90	100	110	120
11	11	22	33	44	55	66	77	88	99	110	121	132
12	12	24	36	48	60	72	84	96	108	120	132	144

Notes

Notes

Notes

Notes

A+ National Pre-accreditation Maths & Literacy for Beauty Therapy 9780170190763